Being Your Best at Baseball

NEL YOMTOV

Children's Press®
An Imprint of Scholastic Inc.

Content Consultant
Barry Wilner
Associated Press
New York City, New York

Library of Congress Cataloging-in-Publication Data
Names: Yomtov, Nelson.
Title: Being your best at baseball / by Nel Yomtov.
Description: New York : Children's Press An Imprint of Scholastic Inc., 2016.
| ? 2017. | Series: A True Book | Includes bibliographical references and
index.
Identifiers: LCCN 2015048507| ISBN 9780531232620 (library binding) | ISBN
9780531236130 (paperback)
Subjects: LCSH: Baseball—Juvenile literature. | Baseball—History—Juvenile
literature.
Classification: LCC GV867.5 .Y66 2016 | DDC 796.357—dc23
LC record available at http://lccn.loc.gov/2015048507

Front cover: A little league celebrating
Back cover: A baseman throwing the ball

Find the Truth!

Everything you are about to read is true *except* for one of the sentences on this page.

Which one is **TRUE**?

T or F The dimensions of every baseball field are the same.

T or F A baseball field is called a diamond.

Find the answers in this book.

3

Contents

THE **BIG** TRUTH!

The All-American Girls Professional Baseball League

Dorothy Harrell in the All-American Girls
Professional Baseball League

4

A pitcher throws a pitch.

Fastball grip

In baseball slang, home plate is called "the dish."

Kids play baseball in the street in Trinidad.

Play Ball!

Millions of people around the world play and enjoy the game of baseball. The sport developed in the United States in the mid-1800s. Within a few decades, it grew to become America's national pastime. People play baseball in backyards and neighborhood **sandlots**. They play in crowd-packed Major League Baseball (MLB) stadiums and international tournaments. You can play, too! With practice and dedication, you will be the best baseball player you can be.

Tools of the Trade

Playing baseball requires some basic equipment. You'll need a bat, a ball, and a baseball mitt, or glove. Wear lightweight clothing that allows you to move freely. Long pants protect your legs when sliding into base or diving for that catch. If you play on grass, wear baseball cleats. They give you the traction, or grip, you'll need to make quick starts and sudden turns.

Glove

Long pants

Cleats

Lightweight clothing

Cleats give you the grip you need to run, jump, turn—or steal a base.

Excellent teamwork can help win a game.

Bring It On

Baseball players come in all shapes and sizes. Good eye-hand **coordination**, a positive attitude, and the ability to be a great teammate can be more important than strength or speed. Baseball is known as a "thinking person's" game. It requires a keen sense of playing "in the moment" and the ability to think ahead.

Take the Field!

A baseball field has an infield with four bases. The outfield extends from the infield to the field boundary. A field's size depends on the level of play. Distances between the bases, and from home plate to the pitcher's mound and to the outfield fences are longest on professional fields. Little League fields are much smaller. Fields are made of grass and dirt or of **synthetic** turf.

 Dodger Stadium in California is the largest in the major leagues. It seats 56,000 people.

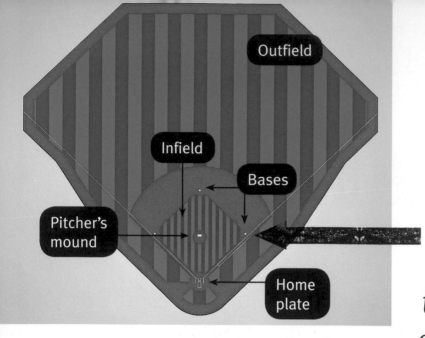

Outfield

Infield

Bases

Pitcher's mound

Home plate

A baseball field is also called a diamond because the infield is diamond-shaped.

On the Diamond

The action on a baseball field starts at the pitcher's mound. The pitcher throws pitches from a rectangular rubber slab on the mound. This "rubber" is 60 feet 6 inches (18.4 meters) from home plate on a professional field. The bases are 90 feet (27.4 m) apart. Distances from home plate to the outfield fences vary. The minimum is 325 feet (99 m) down the right and left sides of the field and 400 feet (122 m) to center field.

Two teams of nine players play a game. The nine players consist of a pitcher; catcher; first, second, and third basemen; shortstop; and left, center, and right fielders. While one team is on the field playing these positions, the opposing team is at bat. Batters score runs by hitting the ball, running the bases, and making it back to home plate. The team with the most runs wins.

Each time a player safely reaches home plate, a team scores one run.

Every MLB bat must be made of one piece of wood.

CHAPTER 3

Rules and Regulations

Baseball is a simple game, but it has many rules. A professional ball game consists of nine innings. In each inning, one team pitches and fields while the other team bats. When the batting team makes three outs, the teams switch places. After nine innings, if there's no tie, the game is over. The team with the most runs at the end of the game is the winner.

You're Out!

How might a batter make an out?

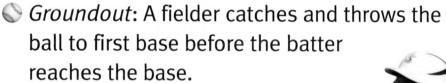 *Strikeout*: A batter earns a strike by either swinging at a pitch and missing, or not swinging at a pitch that lands in the **strike zone**. Three strikes and the batter is out.

Fly out: A fielder catches a batted ball before it touches the ground.

Groundout: A fielder catches and throws the ball to first base before the batter reaches the base.

Tagged out: A base runner is off a base and is tagged with the ball.

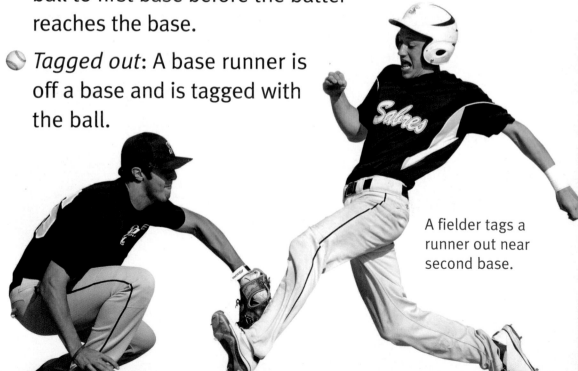

A fielder tags a runner out near second base.

An umpire calls a runner safe at third base.

Safe!

There are a few common ways for a batter to reach first base.

- 🔘 *Hit*: The runner hits the ball and makes it safely to the base.

- 🔘 *Walk*: If a pitch lands outside the strike zone and the batter doesn't swing, the pitch is a "ball." After four balls, the batter walks safely to first base.

- 🔘 *Hit by the pitch*: A thrown pitch strikes the batter, earning the batter a walk.

- 🔘 *Error*: A fielder makes a mistake that allows the hitter to reach base.

- 🔘 *Fielder's choice*: The fielding team tags out another base runner, allowing the batter to reach first base.

New rules force both runners and catchers to be more careful about colliding with each other at home plate.

Some Basic Rules

Rules ensure fair play. Some rules protect players' safety. Batters and runners cannot purposely block the opponent from making a play for the ball. Similarly, fielders cannot block a hitter's swing or interfere with a runner's progress. In 2014, the MLB introduced new rules to help prevent collisions at home plate. Runners cannot go out of their way to run into a catcher. Also, a catcher can only block a runner if the catcher has the ball.

Enforcement on the Field

Four umpires enforce the rules at each MLB game. They usually wear recognizable blue or black shirts. The home plate umpire stands behind the catcher. The other three are positioned near the other three bases. The home plate umpire "calls" strikes, balls, and plays at home plate. He also judges fair and foul balls until they reach first or third base. The base umpires make all decisions regarding the bases.

The All-American Girls Professional Baseball League

The United States entered World War II in 1941. Dozens of professional ballplayers left to serve in the armed forces. Philip K. Wrigley, owner of the Chicago Cubs, wanted to keep people coming to games.
He founded a women's league in 1943 that became the All-American Girls Professional Baseball League (AAGPBL).

Philip K. Wrigley (left) and Charles Grimm of the Chicago Cubs, 1934

AAGPBL rules were very similar to those in the MLB. However, AAGPBL players ran, jumped, and slid in skirts. Extra rules defined proper behavior, beauty routines, and dress codes on and off the field.

Margaret Callaghan sliding home against catcher Dorothy "Dottie" Green

By 1948, a single game could attract a million fans. Managers kept the games exciting by making sure the teams were evenly matched. As a result, competition between the teams was fierce—and fun to watch.

Dorothy Harrell of the Rockford Peaches

More than 600 women played before the AAGPBL ended in 1954. The 1992 film *A League of Their Own* tells the story of the league's beginnings.

Rockford Peaches with manager

Whether at bat or in the field, playing baseball requires skill and concentration.

Hitting, Fielding, and Pitching

In baseball, there are five basic skills that are more important to have than any other. These are running, throwing, hitting, hitting power, and fielding (playing a position on the field). Most baseball players shine in particular skills on this list.

Players who combine all five basic skills are called "five-tool" players.

Types of Hitters

Power hitters, or sluggers, drive the ball long distances. Often, they hit home runs and other hits that allow a player to move more than one base. Because they focus more on power than hitting singles, sluggers are more likely to miss the ball. As a result, they may have a low **batting average**. Line drive hitters hit with less power, but can drive the ball between outfielders for extra bases.

Line drive hitters are also called "spray hitters" because they hit the ball to all fields.

Power hitter Giancarlo Stanton breaks his bat making a hit.

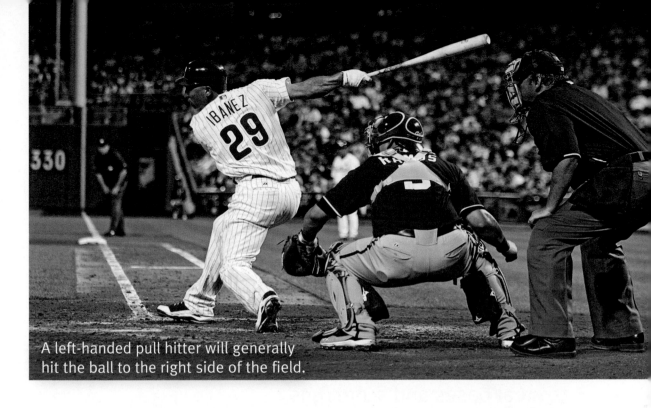
A left-handed pull hitter will generally hit the ball to the right side of the field.

Slap hitters rarely hit for power. Instead, they have excellent bat control and "slap" the ball past infielders to reach base. Pull hitters generally hit the ball to the same side of the field as the side of home plate they stand on. For example, a right-handed batter stands to the left of home plate. He or she would hit the ball to the left side of the field. Opposite field hitters bat the ball in the opposite way.

"Speed Burners"

Some members of a team are particularly quick on their feet. Ballplayers who rely on their ability to run fast are baseball's "speed burners." These speedy players often walk, bunt, or make hits to the infield to reach first base. Once on base, they do what they can to upset the concentration of the opposing team. Speed burners are always trying to steal bases and score runs.

Timeline of the History of Baseball

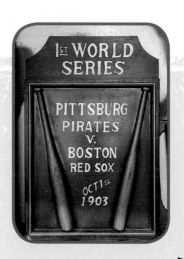

1845
Alexander Joy Cartwright creates the rules of baseball.

1903
The first World Series takes place. The Boston Red Sox beat the Pittsburgh Pirates.

"Good Field, No Hit"

Great fielders who aren't as good at bat are called "good field, no hit" ballplayers. Still, these players are extremely valuable. Scoring many runs is important, but so is preventing the other team from scoring. This part of the game—the **defense**—is where excellent fielders excel. They catch balls and make strong, accurate throws better than other players. Many experts agree that baseball is a game of defense. Great defense helps win games.

1933
The first All-Star game, played by the best professional players in baseball, takes place.

1947
Jackie Robinson breaks baseball's color barrier as the first black major league player in the 20th century.

Kings of the Hill

Great defense begins with solid pitching. There are different types of pitchers. Power pitchers throw balls at speeds of up to 100 miles (161 kilometers) per hour. These pitchers are also called fireballers or flamethrowers. **Finesse** pitchers are sometimes called junk pitchers. They throw relatively slower pitches, such as curveballs or **changeups**. Finesse pitchers focus on disrupting a hitter's timing.

A relief pitcher is one who replaces another pitcher because of injury, fatigue, or ineffectiveness.

Pitchers learn to throw a variety of pitches.

These photos show the standard grip for a fastball (left) and curveball (right).

Get a Grip!

Pitchers throw different kinds of pitches by changing their grip on the baseball. The fastball and the curveball are the two most common types. The fastball is the hardest thrown and the fastest of all pitches. It zooms toward home plate in a straight line with little or no curve. The curveball drops and breaks, or moves to the side, about 13 to 16 feet (4 to 5 m) before reaching home plate.

Play Like the Pros

The best way to sharpen your baseball skills is to get out on the field and play. The more you practice, the better you will understand the game. You will not only improve your skills but also learn the importance of teamwork and good sportsmanship. With some time and hard work, you're sure to become the best player you can be.

 Roughly 2.4 million children in more than 80 countries play Little League baseball.

Hitting

Great hitting begins with a good stance. Stand with knees bent, facing the plate. Your weight should be on your back foot. Hold the bat back and look at the pitcher. At the pitch, shift your weight to the front foot. Stride toward the ball and move your hands forward. Swing the bat with your front arm extended in a smooth motion. Follow through, continuing with the swing's **momentum** after hitting the ball.

Good technique can give a lot of power to your swing.

Pitching

Begin a pitch by standing on the pitching rubber with both feet pointing toward home plate. Hold the ball in your glove with both hands. Rock the foot opposite your throwing arm straight back and turn your hips. As your weight shifts back, lift your front knee. Take the ball with your throwing hand. Stride toward home plate, releasing the ball as your body drives forward, and follow through.

Mo'ne Davis is the first girl to pitch a shutout—allowing no runs—in a Little League World Series game.

You may need to leap for the ball as it flies by.

Fielding and Throwing

As a fielder, keep your weight on the balls of your feet. Be ready to move quickly to either side, or move in or back. To catch a ground ball, bend and put your open glove to the ground. Keep your eyes on the ball until it's securely in your glove. Catch fly balls slightly above head level. The free hand should support the glove hand from behind.

After fielding the ball, you'll want to make a strong, accurate throw. Grip the ball in one hand with your index and middle fingers on top and thumb on the bottom. The ball shouldn't touch your palm. Turn your non-throwing side toward your target, bend your knees, and pull your throwing arm back. Step toward the target and release the ball as you push off your back foot. Follow through toward your target.

Complete a throw by following through. Don't stop your movement once you let go.

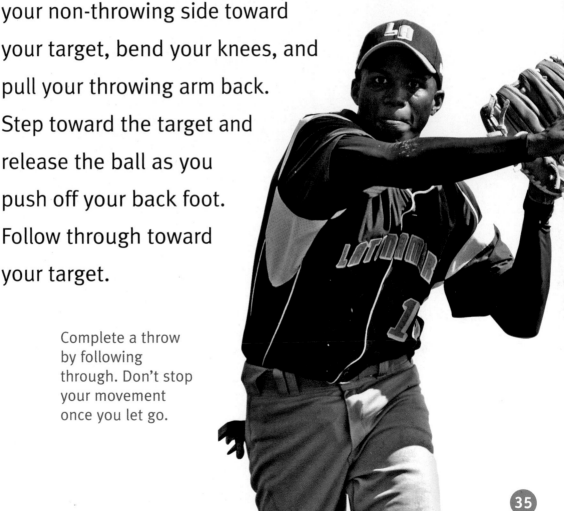

Slide with one leg forward, reaching for the base.

Base Running

Good base running requires awareness and a willingness to take smart risks. When on base, always know where the opposing players are positioned. Are they fast? Do they have strong throwing arms? If you decide to steal a base, wait until the pitcher is well into his or her windup. Pivot on your right leg and drive off your left to start. Run low and fast. Slide into the base with your right leg extended.

Championships

The World Series is the yearly MLB championship series in North America. First played in 1903, it is a best-of-seven series of games played between the top American team and the top National League team. The World Baseball Classic (WBC) is an international baseball tournament. It began in 2006 and is played every four years. Many MLB players participate in the WBC, for either the American team or the team that represents their home country.

World Series trophy

Pitching a "no hitter," when the other team has no hits, is rare. The Baseball Hall of Fame proudly displays the pitchers who managed the feat—along with their baseballs.

CHAPTER 6

The Cream of the Crop

About 16,000 people have played professional baseball since its beginning nearly 150 years ago. These players include the all-time legendary greats as well as today's superstars. Many of the game's best players are members of the Baseball Hall of Fame in Cooperstown, New York. Let's take a quick look at baseball's cream of the crop, past and present.

As of 2016, there are 312 elected members of the Baseball Hall of Fame.

Willie Mays played center field for the Giants, first in New York City, then in San Francisco, California.

Five-Tool Superstars

Willie Mays, Mickey Mantle, and Hank Aaron are among history's greatest five-tool players. Mays hit 660 home runs and stole 338 bases in his career. Mantle hit 536 home runs, won three Most Valuable Player (MVP) awards, and helped win seven World Series. Aaron hit 755 home runs and holds the career record of 2,297 **runs batted in**. Bryce Harper is one of today's brightest stars. In his first four major league seasons, Harper won Rookie of the Year and MVP awards.

Mound Dominators

Sandy Koufax had a blazing fastball and a nasty curve. In the 1960s, Koufax led National League pitchers in wins and strikeouts four times and in **earned run average** five times. He won three Cy Young awards as best pitcher and one MVP award. Clayton Kershaw is considered a modern-day Koufax. Since 2011,  Kershaw has won three Cy Young awards and an MVP award. He also led National League pitchers in earned run average four straight years.

Sandy Koufax also excelled at basketball, winning a college scholarship in the sport.

41

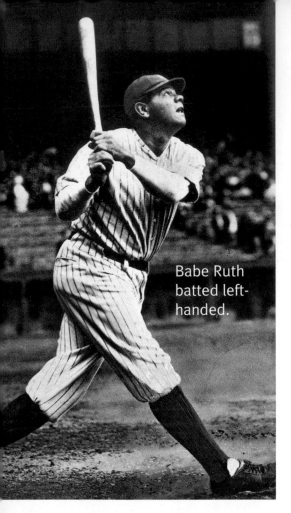

Babe Ruth batted left-handed.

Before Babe Ruth, the Yankees had never won a World Series. With him, they won four.

Pure Hitters

Babe Ruth began as a successful pitcher and later switched to the outfield. He was the greatest home run hitter ever, leading the American League 12 times. He held the home run record with 714, until Hank Aaron passed that mark in 1974. Ty Cobb led the American League in batting average 12 times and has the all-time highest career average, .366. Ted Williams hit 521 career home runs and batted .344.

Barrier Breakers

In 1947, Jackie Robinson became the first African American major league ballplayer since the 1880s. Robinson was one of the finest players of his time. During his 10-year career, he batted .311 and won Rookie of the Year and MVP awards. Lavone "Pepper" Paire Davis was a catcher and infielder in the All-American Girls Professional Baseball League. Davis was an outstanding fielder and line drive hitter. She was also a member of the 1946 AAGPBL champion Racine Belles. All of these players are great examples of being your best at baseball ★

Jackie Robinson slides into home plate.

Most runs scored in a nine-inning game by two teams: 30, by the Texas Rangers and Baltimore Orioles (2007)

Most seasons played in major leagues by a player: 27, by Nolan Ryan

Most games won in a single season by a single team: 116, by the Seattle Mariners (2001) and Chicago Cubs (1906)

Most consecutive games played by a player: 2,632, by Cal Ripken (1982 to 1998)

Highest home attendance in a single season: 4,483,350, for the Colorado Rockies (1993)

Highest lifetime career batting average: .366, by Ty Cobb

Fastest recorded pitch in baseball history: 105.1 mph (169 kph), by Aroldis Chapman (2010)

Did you find the truth?

F The dimensions of every baseball field are the same.

T A baseball field is called a diamond.

Resources

Books

Chen, Albert. *Baseball: Intel on Today's Biggest Stars and Tips on How to Play Like Them*. New York: Time Home Entertainment, 2012.

Jacobs, Greg, and Joe Gergen. *The Everything Kids' Baseball Book*. Avon, MA: Adams Media, 2014.

Kelley, K. C. *Baseball Superstars 2015*. New York: Scholastic, 2015.

Visit this Scholastic Web site for more information on being your best at baseball:

★ www.factsfornow.scholastic.com

Enter the keywords **Being Your Best at Baseball**

Important Words

batting average (BAT-ing AV-ur-ij) a number in baseball that shows how often a batter earns a hit that results in reaching base

changeups (CHAYNJ-ups) slow pitches thrown in a way that tricks the batter

coordination (koh-or-dih-NAY-shuhn) the ability to make your arms and legs work well together

defense (di-FENS) the side in sports that tries to prevent the other team from scoring

earned run average (URND RUN AV-ur-ij) the number of earned runs a pitcher gives up every nine innings

finesse (fin-ESS) skill and cleverness that is shown in the way someone deals with a situation or problem

momentum (moh-MEN-tuhm) force or speed that something gains when it is moving

runs batted in (RUNZ BAT-id IN) a statistic that credits a batter for allowing a runner or himself to score

sandlots (SAND-lots) pieces of unoccupied land, often used by children for games

strike zone (STRIKE ZOHN) an area over home plate extending from the batter's armpits to the knees

synthetic (sin-THET-ik) manufactured or human made, rather than found in nature

Index

Page numbers in **bold** indicate illustrations.

About the Author

Nel Yomtov is an award-winning author with a passion for writing nonfiction books for young readers. He has written books and graphic novels about history, geography, science, and other subjects. Nel has worked at Marvel Comics, where he edited, wrote, and colored hundreds of titles. He has also served as editorial director of a children's book publisher and as publisher of Hammond World Atlas books.

Yomtov lives in the New York City area with his wife, Nancy, a teacher. Their son, Jess, is a sports journalist.